Life in the Old West

WOMEN OF THE WEST

Bobbie Kalman & Jane Lewis

Crabtree Publishing Company

www.crabtreebooks.com

LIFE IN THE OLD WEST

Created by Bobbie Kalman

To Debbie, Julie, Lisa, and Heather—
Women of the Bookstore!

Editor-in-Chief
Bobbie Kalman

Writing team
Bobbie Kalman
Jane Lewis

Researcher
Amelinda Berube

Managing editor
Lynda Hale

Editors
Kate Calder
Heather Levigne

Copy editors
Niki Walker
Hannelore Sotzek

Photo research
Jane Lewis
Hannelore Sotzek

Special thanks to
William A. Hastings, Littleton Historical Museum;
Linda Eade, Yosemite Research Library; The CRB
Foundation Heritage Project; Lee Summers, Wilder
Ranch State Park; Robert C. Grace, Unit Ranger,
William B. Ide Adobe State Historic Park; Spring
Mountain Ranch State Park; Jim Bowman, Glenbow
Archives, Calgary

Computer design
Lynda Hale
Campbell Creative Services (cover)

Production coordinator
Hannelore Sotzek

Separations and film
Dot 'n Line Image Inc.

Printer
Worzalla Publishing Company

Crabtree Publishing Company

www.crabtreebooks.com   1-800-387-7650

Cataloging-in-Publication Data
Kalman, Bobbie
    Women of the west
(Life in the Old West)
Includes index.
ISBN 0-7787-0080-1 (library bound) ISBN 0-7787-0112-3 (pbk.) This book describes the lives and
experiences of women in the nineteenth-century North American west, including immigrants,
African Americans, and Native Americans. 1. Women pioneers—West (North America)—History—
19th century—Juvenile literature. 2. Women—West (North America)—History—19th century—
Juvenile literature. 3. Frontier and pioneer life—West (North America)—Juvenile literature. 4. West
(North America)—Social life and customs—Juvenile literature. [1. Frontier and pioneer life—West
(North America). 2. Women—West (North America)—History. 3. West (North America)—Social
life and customs.] I. Lewis, Jane. II. Title. III. Series: Kalman, Bobbie. Life in the Old West.
F596.K359 1999   j920.72'0978   LC 99-23492
                                                                                       CIP

**Published in
the United States**
PMB 16A
350 Fifth Ave.
Suite 3308
New York, NY
10118

**Published
in Canada**
616 Welland Ave.,
St. Catharines,
Ontario, Canada
L2M 5V6

**Published in the
United Kingdom**
73 Lime Walk
Headington
Oxford
0X3 7AD
United Kingdom

**Published
in Australia**
386 Mt. Alexander Rd.,
Ascot Vale (Melbourne)
V1C 3032

TABLE OF CONTENTS

THE WESTERN FRONTIER

In the mid-1800s, people who lived in eastern North America began moving west. Many adventurous men and women traveled across the continent to the unsettled wilderness known as the **western frontier**. The first settlers made the long journey in **covered wagons**. After railway lines were built, most people traveled by train. The journey was only the first of many challenges for these western pioneers.

Too risky for women?

In the beginning, the travelers to the West were mostly men. The trip was full of hardships and dangers, and the frontier was a difficult and lonely place to live. Some people believed that it was too risky for women to make the journey. Many women were excited about the new land, however, and did not want to be left behind. They began to head west as well.

*Pioneers moved west for many reasons. Many were attracted by offers of inexpensive land and reports of mild weather. Some people went to join relatives who had already moved there. Others hoped to find gold during the **gold rushes**.*

Women in the West

Over the years, many women made the journey to the West. Some moved with their family, and others went on their own. Single women arrived on the frontier in search of work, adventure, or a husband. Many relied on their money, skills, and determination to start a business or establish a **homestead**. Although western life was difficult, it offered women more freedom and independence than they had known in the East.

WOMEN ON THE MOVE

The overland journey was long and difficult for the early settlers heading west. These hardy pioneers crossed the continent in covered wagons pulled by horses, mules, or oxen. The trip took many months. For safety, the settlers traveled in groups of covered wagons called **wagon trains**.

Many people in the East believed that hard, physical jobs should be done by men. They thought that women were not smart or strong enough to do such work. On a wagon train, however, there was so much to do that men did not worry about who did what—it was more important that the work was done! Women proved that they were willing and able to do work that was usually reserved for men.

Bad weather was one of many obstacles that westward travelers faced on their journey. This wagon train is struggling through muddy trails in a heavy rainstorm.

Women's work

Women had many responsibilities on the journey. They gathered fuel for campfires, cooked meals, washed and mended clothing, and cared for those who were sick. Women also drove wagons, loaded and unloaded belongings, tended animals, pitched tents, and looked after the children. A woman whose husband became ill or died along the way had to get her family and wagon to the West by herself.

A long, slow walk

The pioneers brought wagons on their journey, but they usually did not ride in them. The wagons were full of belongings and had little room for passengers. If people sat in the wagon, it became too heavy for the animals to pull for long periods of time. Riding in a wagon over bumpy ground was uncomfortable for the passengers. For these reasons, people often walked alongside the wagon train.

Many women gave birth during their westward journey. The wagons stopped rolling for one day when the baby arrived. If the new mother was not well and ready to walk again by the next day, she and the baby rode in the wagon.

At the Homestead

When the settlers finally arrived at their destination, they found that most of the land was wilderness. They had to chop down trees and remove rocks and tree stumps before they could build a home or plant crops. Most farms were miles away from any neighbor, so a family did all the work on its own. Once a family established a homestead, there was plenty of work to do to keep it running. Women worked from sunrise to sunset every day to help their family survive.

Food for the family

There were few stores, if any, where settlers could purchase food, so preparing a meal took a great deal of time and effort. Pioneers fetched water from a well or nearby stream because there was no indoor plumbing. They raised or grew all their food. Families kept chickens and cows for eggs, milk, and meat, and planted herbs, vegetables, and fruit trees. Women cooked the family's meals in the fireplace or on a wood stove.

*This woman is gathering dried grass for the roof of her new home on the Plains. She and her husband are building a house out of **sod**, or earth. Their "soddy" will keep the family cool in the summer and warm in the winter.*

Handmade clothing

Pioneer women made and mended most of the family's clothes. First, they spun wool and **flax** with a spinning wheel and wove it into fabric. They then sewed the fabric by hand into clothing. They also knitted socks, sweaters, and hats from the wool they spun. Making clothing was time-consuming, so settlers rarely threw away old clothes. Instead, women patched and mended every piece of clothing many times to get more use out of it.

Laundry was another lengthy task. Women boiled water over a fire or on the stove and then scrubbed their clothing by hand in large tubs. They rinsed the laundry in cold water and hung it to dry.

Making supplies

Women made soap and candles from scratch. Each of these jobs took a full day. Soap was made from a mixture of **tallow**, or melted animal fat, and a strong, burning chemical called **lye**. The mixture was boiled and then poured into a mold to harden.

Candle making was a task that children could help with. Settler families made candles by dipping a **wick**, or string, into hot tallow and then letting it dry and harden. They dipped the wick several times until the candles were thick enough to burn for hours.

*The first step in making clothing was to shear the sheep. Women then combed the fleece, spun it into wool, and wound it into **skeins**, or loose coils. They knitted sweaters and wove fabric for sewing from this wool.*

*Women's many chores included feeding livestock, churning butter, baking bread, canning fruit and vegetables, and **preserving** meat.*

WORKING ON A RANCH

Some pioneer families started **ranches**, or large farms, in the West. They raised sheep or cattle to sell in eastern markets. Ranch women not only looked after their home and family, but they also helped run the business.

Cowgirls

Some women worked as **hired hands**, or paid workers, on larger ranches. They were known as **cowgirls**. Cowgirls rode the range alongside the cowboys, herding and roping cattle, fixing buildings and fences, harvesting hay, and looking after the **livestock**.

This cowgirl works on a large ranch. On most days, she looks after cattle out on the wide, open grazing area called the range.

Ranch jobs

Women often handled the ranch's **accounts**. They kept track of animals that were bought and sold and paid the hired hands. They also fed livestock, milked cows, and cleaned out dirty barn stalls. Women **branded** cattle, plowed fields, and threshed and baled hay. If a woman's husband became ill or died, she was in charge of running the entire ranch.

(right) This woman is bringing a drink of water to the hired hands who work on her ranch during the fall harvest.

(below) Mrs. Buckley and her daughters had no trouble running the ranch while Mr. Buckley was away.

RAISING A FAMILY

This couple has just started to raise a family. Like most pioneer families, their two children will probably have many more brothers and sisters in the years to come.

In addition to the many difficulties and hard work involved in maintaining a homestead, women were responsible for taking care of their family. Men were often busy working outside the home, so pioneer women had to rely on their own courage and strength to bear and raise children on the frontier.

Bearing children

Being pregnant was not easy for settler women. With so many jobs to do around the homestead, a pregnant woman could not afford to take time to rest unless she was seriously ill. She often continued working up to the day she gave birth. Giving birth was not easy, either. In the nineteenth century, babies were born at home. A woman sometimes had only her husband and children to help her. Doctors or **midwives** had to travel long distances to reach the homestead. They often did not arrive there until after the baby was born.

Child care

After the birth of a child, a mother had even more work to do! She did all her daily chores and looked after her new baby, too. A woman with many children was fortunate because the older children could help with the baby and other jobs around the homestead. If there were older adults in the household, such as aunts, uncles, or grandparents, they also helped the mother look after the children.

Many western families were large. Some households had as many as eight children or more. This older brother must have felt somewhat outnumbered among all these girls!

Life in the western wilderness was not only challenging, it was often hazardous. Bad weather, fires, illness, accidents, loneliness, and the death of loved ones were some of the problems that pioneer women faced.

Dangerous animals

The threat of wild animals was another big problem. Foxes stole chickens and eggs, and groundhogs and skunks ate vegetables from the garden. Some animals could be dangerous. When startled, bears, wildcats, and rattlesnakes often attacked people. Many women learned to use a gun to protect their family and food supply. Mrs. Smith, shown left, shot a wildcat that was lurking too close to her homestead!

Loneliness

Most pioneers left behind friends and family when they moved west. They often settled in areas where the nearest neighbors were miles away. Living on an isolated homestead caused some women to feel lonely and homesick.

Fear of attack

Many settlers made their home in areas where Native Americans lived. Although some pioneers were able to live on friendly terms with their Native neighbors, others could not. Many settlers were hostile towards the Native people and took over their land without any respect for Native rights. As a result, some groups of Native Americans felt that they had no choice but to fight the settlers in order to survive. Such disputes caused many women to live in fear that their home and family might be attacked.

Tragedy

Even in peaceful times, frontier life was rugged and dangerous. Accidents, illness, and diseases were common. Babies and children were especially at risk of becoming ill. Many settlers died at an early age because their homesteads were too far from a doctor or town hospital. If a woman's husband died, she had to support her children on her own.

JOBS FOR WOMEN

As more settlers arrived in the West, towns quickly developed. Excellent job opportunities awaited women who moved to these towns. Most of the first settlers were men who were not used to cooking, cleaning, sewing, or doing laundry. Many of the women who lived in the West made their living by providing these services. They found jobs in restaurants, shops, or hotels.

Businesswomen

Some women preferred not to work for anyone else and established their own business. They opened hat shops, clothing shops, restaurants, bakeries, hotels, boarding houses, and laundry services. Many women bought land or staked **mining claims** during the gold rushes and worked as **prospectors**. Some even hired men to prospect for them!

Teaching was a common job for unmarried women in the nineteenth century. Teachers often started working when they were only fifteen or sixteen years old. Some women also found jobs caring for the children of wealthier families.

These women opened a restaurant and made money to support their families by selling food to miners and other workers who wanted a home-cooked meal. Will the little boy grow up to be a miner or a cook?

Mrs. Tyler earned a living as a photographer. She found a creative way to advertise her business!

Many immigrant women who moved to the West worked as cooks or laundresses.

LEISURE TIME

Since women had such a great deal of work to do, there was little time for leisure. When they did get a moment of rest, many spent their time doing something that was productive as well as relaxing. Much of their spare time was taken up with jobs such as spinning, quilting, and needlework. Women produced beautiful and useful items for their homes or to give away as gifts.

Combining work and fun

Hard work was easier when it was done with friends! Several women worked together on big jobs such as husking corn, preserving food, or making candles and soap. These work "parties" were called **bees**. Women also had bees to sew, knit, and quilt. Organizing work into group activities was fun and gave women a chance to visit and exchange news with friends and neighbors.

These women have gathered for a quilting bee. The quilt is a gift for a young woman in the community who is getting married. The bride will need many things for her new home.

Writing

Women spent some of their spare time writing letters to friends and relatives who lived far away. They sent news about their home and family to loved ones in the East. Women also kept **journals**, or diaries, in which they recorded their experiences and the events of daily life. Those journals are valuable to us today—they tell us what it was like to live on the frontier.

Reading

Many women enjoyed reading magazines, novels, and newspapers. These items were expensive and scarce, so if a woman owned a book or magazine, she read it over and over again. Letters from relatives and friends were saved and re-read many times, as well.

(above) If there were neighbors nearby, women sometimes got together for tea. Visiting provided a break from hard work on the homestead!

M ost pioneer women brought simple, comfortable dresses to their new western home. They needed practical clothing for living and working at a homestead in the wilderness or in a town with dusty, unpaved roads. Their garments had to last a long time, too. In the early years there were few stores on the frontier where settlers could buy ready-made clothing. If new clothing was needed, it had to be made by hand.

*(top) Most women wore long skirts all the time, making it awkward to work in the fields! They also wore hats or **bonnets** to shade their face from the sun.*
(left) Settler women usually had one good dress to wear to church and social events.

The problem with skirts

In the nineteenth century, people believed that it was improper for women to expose their legs or ankles. For this reason, women wore long skirts. In the West, however, long skirts quickly became dirty. The hems dragged along the ground while women worked outdoors. Dresses were soiled even indoors because many frontier homes had dirt floors. Long skirts also made riding a horse difficult. A woman wearing a long skirt had to ride **sidesaddle**, with both legs on one side of a horse's body. Riding sidesaddle was awkward and impractical for doing chores around a farm or ranch.

Making adjustments

Since dresses were the fashion at the time, many women began wearing clothing that resembled dresses but was more practical. **Culottes**, or wide-legged trousers that looked like a skirt, became popular. Women who wore them were able to ride a horse **astride**, with one leg on each side. Culottes made it easier for women to do many jobs. Some women wore **bloomers**, or loose trousers with a short skirt over top. Although bloomers were practical, they were not very popular. The idea of women wearing short skirts was difficult for many people to accept.

Cowgirl attire

Women who worked on a ranch often wore the same clothing as that worn by cowboys. It was much easier to ride horses, rope cattle, and herd livestock in men's clothing than in traditional women's clothing. Women wore leather **chaps** to protect their pants and a shirt with pockets instead of a blouse. They also wore a **bandanna** around their neck and a wide-brimmed hat for protection from the sun.

This cowgirl posed for a photograph in her culottes, bandanna, and hat.

(left) A wealthy townswoman might have dressed like this. (right) Many people thought that bloomers were indecent.

GROWING UP IN THE WEST

irls who grew up in the West led a much different life from those in the East. Most eastern girls learned music, dancing, sewing, and **etiquette**. Etiquette required them to be polite, soft-spoken, and cheerful. Being "ladylike" was not a priority on the frontier, however. Independence, determination, and a willingness to work hard were considered important qualities in western women.

Never too young

Children started doing chores at age four or five. Young girls cleaned, helped prepare meals, and looked after younger children. They also weeded the garden, fed chickens, gathered eggs, and collected wood or **buffalo chips** for the fire. Older girls had more responsibilities. They hunted, tended livestock, milked cows, planted crops, sewed, cooked, and did laundry.

A family affair

Not all girls and women in the West lived on a ranch or farm. Some young girls helped look for gold on their parents' mining claim. Others worked in town at the family business—a hotel, store, or railroad station.

Free to enjoy fun and games

During playtime, boys and girls enjoyed rugged activities—they hiked, explored, swam, and climbed trees. Young girls in the East might not have been allowed to do these things, but western girls had more freedom. They were encouraged to be independent at a young age, which prepared them for life on the frontier.

How many children do you count in this family? What chores do you think each of them did at the homestead?

Toys

Fancy toys were a luxury most western children did not enjoy. Instead, they played with objects such as stones, barrel hoops, sticks, or marbles. Girls' dolls were usually homemade from rags, wood, or dried corn husks. Children jumped rope, played tag, and flew homemade kites. Make-believe was a big part of their games. A little imagination provided hours of fun!

Girls at school

At school, girls learned arithmetic, reading, writing, history, and geography. Some girls, however, were not sent to school. Parents needed their help at the homestead. Some parents also believed that girls did not need an education because they would marry and raise a family instead of having a career.

(right) Two schoolgirls share a secret at lunchtime.
(bottom) Children found all kinds of places to have fun!

IMMIGRANT WOMEN

Many of the women who moved to the West in the mid-1800s were **immigrants**, or people who left their homeland and came to live in North America. They came from places such as Ireland, Italy, Poland, Scandinavia, and China.

Land of opportunity

Some immigrants arrived in western North America in search of work. They hoped to earn money and then return home with their savings. Others came to live permanently in a new country. Many moved with their family to escape war or other poor living conditions in their country. Some families came to North America because they wanted the freedom to practice their religion, which they did not have at home.

Hard times

Although there were many opportunities for immigrants in the West, life was not easy for newcomers. Most immigrant women spoke little English, so they could not communicate well with their neighbors. Their beliefs and traditions seemed strange to other settlers who were not familiar with their customs. As a result, it was difficult for them to make friends. Life in the West was often lonely for immigrant women.

The Doukhobors were a religious group that immigrated to Canada from Russia. Doukhobor women did hard, physical work in the fields when the men were working away from home. The women below are pulling a plow.

African American Women

Many African Americans moved west in the mid-1800s. Some arrived after gaining freedom or escaping from **slavery** in the United States. They came to the frontier because it was illegal to own slaves there. Others were brought to the West as slaves by their white "owners." Many of those African Americans fought for, and earned, their freedom after they arrived.

A new start

Some African American women went alone to the frontier. Most of them settled in towns and worked as laundresses, housekeepers, cooks, or nurses. African American women who became wealthy were able to use their money to bring other former slaves to the West. Many women tried to locate family members who were separated due to slavery.

(right) This woman made her living as a midwife.

(below) Some African American women came with their family and helped establish homesteads in the West.

NATIVE AMERICAN WOMEN

In Native American society, women were treated with honor and respect. A woman's ability to bear children was considered a sacred and powerful gift. In many Native nations, women owned property, played an important role in government, and were respected healers.

Daily life

Depending on where they lived and on the lifestyle of their nation, Native American women were responsible for jobs such as planting and harvesting crops, fetching water, grinding corn, gathering berries, preparing meals, making **tipis**, caring for children, weaving cloth and baskets, making pottery, and **tanning** hides. Women in most Native American nations lived and worked closely together and shared many responsibilities. For example, a few older women watched the children while the rest of the women planted crops.

Helping the settlers

Many Native Americans welcomed the first settlers who came west. They often helped pioneers find their way if a group got lost in unfamiliar territory. Women settlers learned many survival skills from Native American women. Native women taught them how to use the natural resources around them to build their homes and how to find food that grew wild in the areas where they lived.

Terrible times

Many Native people died from diseases carried by settlers, such as smallpox and influenza. The Native Americans suffered another tragedy as well—the loss of their land. The government allowed settlers to take over the land on which the Native Americans lived and claim it for themselves. Settlers also destroyed the major food source of many Native Americans—the buffalo. The nineteenth century was a difficult time for Native American women. They witnessed the destruction of their people, land, and culture.

A clash of cultures

Native American traditions and beliefs were different from those of the pioneers. Most settlers did not understand or respect the Native American way of life. They believed that the Native people needed to be rescued. They tried to change the Native Americans by teaching them to act like the settlers.

In many Native American nations, women were responsible for planting, tending, and harvesting crops, as well as preparing food for their family.

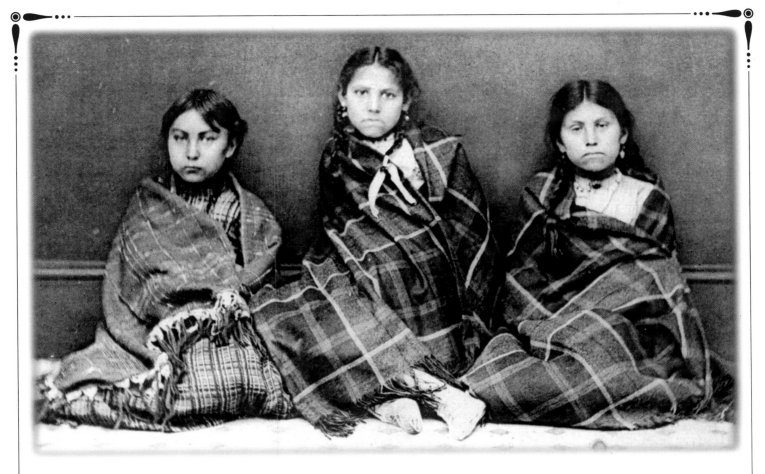

Boarding schools

In an attempt to "help" Native Americans, the government established English-speaking schools, which Native children were forced to attend. Most of these schools were **boarding schools**, where the children lived and studied far away from their family and nation. Native girls were taught how to run a home in the style of settler women. They learned how to cook, clean, dress, and behave like the pioneers. Girls who went to these schools were never accepted by the people in English-speaking society. Those who returned to their nation found that they no longer fit into Native society, either.

(top) These three Native American girls have just arrived at a boarding school.
(right) The girls have now been at school for more than a year. How have they changed? How do you think they felt about being forced to change?

WOMEN'S RIGHTS AND EQUALITY

Until the late 1800s and early 1900s, women were not allowed to own property, vote in elections, or attend college or university. Their opinions were not considered important, so no one asked what they thought about laws or other matters. Most women were expected to stay home and care for their husband, home, and family whether they wanted to or not. A woman was even considered the property of her father or husband! Women's rights, however, changed at the end of the nineteenth century.

Changing laws

People vote to elect officials into the government. These officials make the laws by which we live. At first, men were the only people allowed to vote or run in elections. All the laws were made by men, and many officials were not aware of women's needs. By getting the right to vote, women gained the power to help change laws to reflect their needs as well as men's. This right also allowed them to run for positions in the government.

Getting the vote

Women in the West were the first to vote in North America. In 1869, women in Wyoming gained the right to vote in their territory. Soon after, women in Utah won this right as well. Canadian women were the first to gain the **federal** vote. In 1918, they were allowed to vote for the leader of their country. American women achieved this right in 1920.

Equality in the West

Although many of the ideas about **equality** for women in North America started in the East, they were practiced first in the West. Women on the frontier established their own businesses and homesteads. They successfully did "men's" work and proved themselves to be able, smart, and strong. Many women became respected members of their community.

Some men believed that women should not be allowed to vote and tried to stop them from doing so. Other men agreed that women should have equal rights and supported the women who fought for the right to vote.

REMARKABLE WESTERNERS

Many western women led interesting and unusual lives. These are stories of just a few of those women. When you have finished reading them, write a story about what you would have done if you had lived on the frontier.

Susan La Flesche

Nellie McClung

Susan La Flesche was the first Native American woman to become a doctor. After graduating from medical school in Philadelphia, she returned to her reservation in Nebraska. Susan set up a medical practice there and raised money to build a hospital.

*Nellie McClung was one of Canada's strongest activists for women's **suffrage**, or the right to vote. She worked as a writer and public speaker and gave many speeches in support of women's rights. Nellie helped the women in her province of Manitoba become the first to vote in Canada.*

Biddy Mason

Nellie Cashman

*Biddy Mason earned her freedom from slavery at age 38, in California. She worked as a nurse and bought land with her wages. Biddy made a fortune in **real estate** and used her wealth to help others. She donated to churches and provided food and shelter for people who were homeless.*

Nellie Cashman went to the West in 1869 in search of adventure. She was a successful prospector and found gold in many places in the West. When she was not prospecting, Nellie established and ran hotels, restaurants, and boarding houses. She gave away most of her fortune to hospitals, schools, and churches, and helped many people who needed food, money, or a place to stay.

One of Nellie McClung's most notable and successful ideas was to put on a humorous play mocking the Manitoba government. In the play, men had no rights and pleaded with an all-female government for the right to vote.

GLOSSARY

accounts Records of money that comes in and goes out of a household or business

bandanna A square piece of cotton fabric

bonnet A woman's hat that ties under the chin

branding The act of marking an animal's hide to show ownership

buffalo chips Dried buffalo dung

chaps Leather leggings worn over pants

covered wagon A wagon with a canvas top

equality The condition of one person being treated in the same way as another

etiquette A set of rules about behavior

federal Describing something that refers to a country, as opposed to a state, province, or city

flax A plant that is used to make linen cloth

gold rush A rush of people to a place where gold has been discovered

homestead All the land and buildings that form a pioneer's property

livestock The animals kept on a farm or ranch

midwife A woman who assists other women in childbirth

mining claim A piece of land chosen by a prospector on which he or she searches for gold

preserving The process of preparing food so that it will not spoil

prospector A person who searches for gold and other precious minerals

quilting The process of making a blanket from small pieces of fabric

real estate The business of buying and selling land

slavery The practice of "owning" human beings and forcing them to work without pay

tanning The process of making animal skins into leather

tipi A type of Native American home that is made of buffalo skins

INDEX

ACKNOWLEDGMENTS

Illustrations and colorizations
Barbara Bedell: cover, pages 18, 20, 23, 26, 29, 30
Antoinette "Cookie" Bortolon: page 21
Trevor Morgan: title page
Bonna Rouse: pages 6, 7, 10, 15, 19, 24

Photographs and reproductions
The CRB Foundation Heritage Project/Claude Charlebois: pages 8, 31; Dawson City Museum and Historical Society: page 17 (top); The Denver Public Library, Western History Collection: page 16; Eyewire, Inc.: page 4; Glenbow Archives, Calgary: title page (colorized, black & white original photo), pages 12, 22; Kansas State Historical Society: page 19; courtesy of the Littleton Historical Museum: page 9 (both); Montana Historical Society, Helena/Evelyn J. Cameron: pages 10-11, 11 (top); National Cowboy Hall of Fame, Oklahoma City: page 21; courtesy of the National Park Service: page 5; Nebraska State Historical Society: page 25 (bottom); Oregon Historical Society: page 25 (top) (ORHI23608-a); Collection of Peter E. Palmquist: pages 13, 17 (bottom left); Public Archives Canada: page 20; Smithsonian Institution National Anthropological Archives: page 27 (both) (55516, 55517); The Society of California Pioneers: page 17 (bottom right) (detail, black & white original photo); Division of Special Collections & University Archives, University of Oregon Library System: page 23; Special Collections, University of Washington Libraries/A. Curtis (#19943): page 28; Wyoming Division of Cultural Resources: page 14

6 7 8 9 0   Printed in the U.S.A.   8 7 6 5 4